AF505704

Without You

YouTube Profits

2021

FRANCIS TAN

Without You YouTube Profits 2021

Francis Tan

Content Page

Introduction to "Without You YouTube Profits" Course

Welcome to Without You YouTube Profits Course.

Through this YouTube Profits Course, I'll be showing you for free how to make money without having for you to do the talking or showing your face.(**Without Creating Your Own Video**)

You just need to upload a compilation video and edit it, then share it to your own YouTube channel as your own.

I'll be going through many tips & tricks and great advice through the course.

There are 8 chapters to this course and I hope anyone of you who is keen to monetize from this course can follow through the 8 chapters.

Chapter 1:- How to Install Free Video Editing Software

If you're keen to monetize from uploading compilation YouTube channel, the best way to do it is to edit the video you are going to share on your own channel.

It's very critical to edit the video so that nobody will make a claim on the copyright of the video you are sharing.

In this way they can't claim on the revenues you have generated on the compilation video.

Firstly you have to open up your browser to search for fx home/Hit film Express.

Click Here to install the Hit Film Express Video Editor.

I want to recommend another video editor is Tube Buddy which is equally an excellent option to Hit Film Express.

When the Hit Film Express opens up, you'll have the choice to choose the iOS or Windows version.

Join Our _"Without You Youtube Profits"_ **Support Group**

For me I'll choose the Windows free version (I'm using Windows laptop) then click on the Installer.

You'll receive a download link through your email to install the Hit Film Express video editor software.

Fig. 1 Hit Film Express New

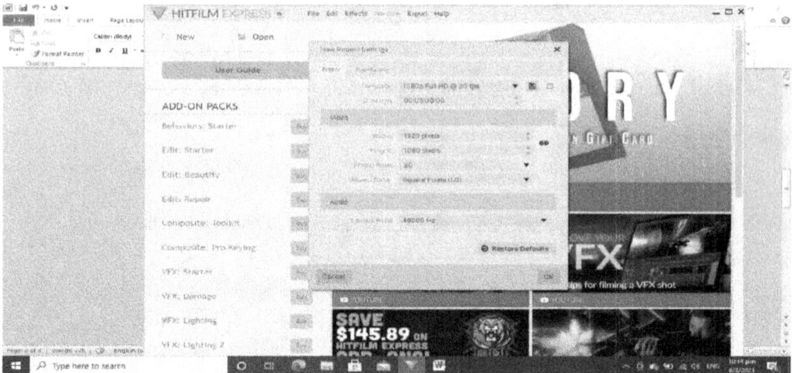

Now you can open up the Hit Film Express video editor, select new from the top left-hand corner and select Project Settings.

Normally my advice is you should choose 1080p full HD X 30 fps. It's much faster to download as compared to 720p full HD 60fps.

At this point, go to YouTube MP4 site to download a compilation video you like.

Copy the link at the search bar and then paste it onto the left pane of the video editor.

On the right-hand pane, you can see 2 bars, the top bar is the Video 1 clip and the bottom bar is Audio 1.

Fig. 2 Hit Film Express

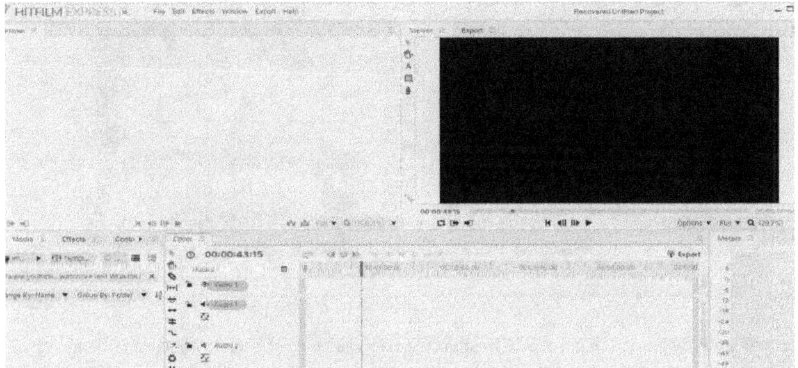

At the bottom left, look for the slider and select, then go to the video clip to slide it to the portion you want to delete.

Go to the editor and select the blade to cut the portion of the clip you've selected.

Drag the rest of the clip to the left to complete the editing.

You might want to edit the audio of the clip by right clicking & selecting the speed duration.

It'll show 100% which is the normal speed; you can choose 10% so that the video clip is shorter, but the audio is faster now but you can add your own music.

ShutterStock

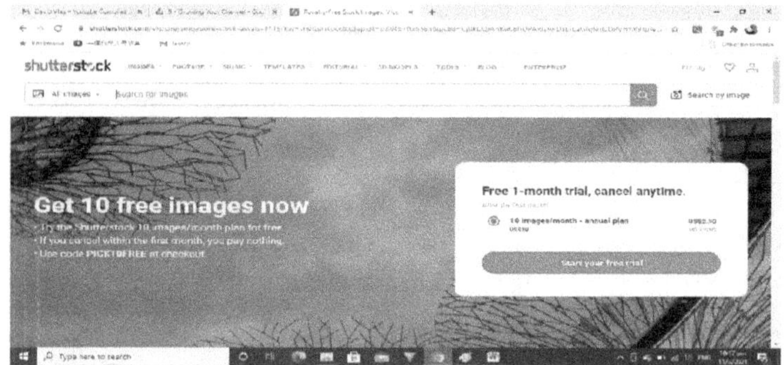

To add your own music, get a 1 month Shutterstock Free Trial Here where you can download non-copyrighted music.

Look out for different genres like happy mood montage and choose the piece you want to download.

Add the music to the left window pane and then drag to the right to become audio 2.

You can adjust the music lower by pulling the audio line lower or louder by pulling audio 2 lines up higher.

To mute any curse word from the video, use the splitter and click on the portion with the curse word & right click to unlink which makes that portion of the clip to be muted.

Join Our "Without You Youtube Profits" Support Group

After you have finished editing the video, go to the top menu and click export.

The edited video file will appear on the top pane of the window where you choose In-Out to select the whole edited video to export.

Then select the "Default Preset" – to 1080p full HD 30fps.

The exporting video file will appear on the bottom pane to show the progress of the exporting.

If it's not progressing, just click start exporting at the bottom menu.

At this point, you can see the edited video is playing on the right side of the screen to let you see it's playing nicely.

Finally, you can save the video file to wherever storage you want and eventually upload to your YouTube channel as your own creation.

P.S:- Stay tune, the next chapter 2 I'll touch on Optimization of Your Channel

Chapter 2:- Optimizing Your YouTube Channel

YouTube Video Analytics

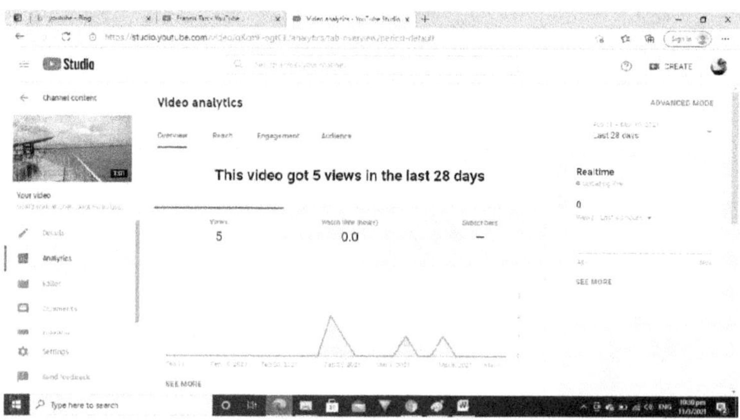

Your goals in creating your own Compilation Videos ultimately are to monetize it and make money.

In order for you to monetize your YouTube Channel, you need to set up your Channel Analytics.

Login to your YouTube channel, go to Analytic ➡ Channel and choose advance, select your location. (e.g. US).

Next go to Channel keywords then type the keywords related to your video in the box.

For example, if your video is related to "Travel", you may add keywords like "exotics", "beautiful beaches" and "good food" & etc.

It's important to have keywords so that whenever people search on YouTube any keywords which are quite similar to yours will open up your video.

Next you want to make sure "Channel recommendations" & "Subscriber counts" are allowed.

Allow channel recommendation is critical so that when other YouTubers like your content, they may strongly recommend it to other viewers.

However, leave the "Disable interest based-ads" untouched in order not to significantly reduce the numbers of Ads in your Channel which correspond to your revenues earned.

Then you save this setting by clicking "Save".

YouTube Channel Branding

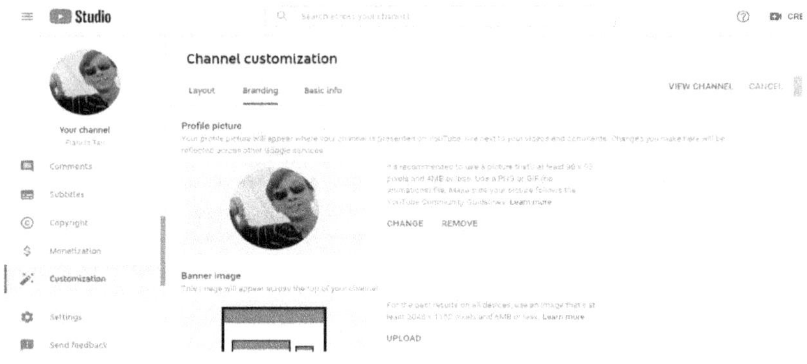

Then go to "Branding" & click on it, a brand watermark window will appear where you can see a watermark on the bottom right corner.

This is where you can add your own photo or your name to let people know you're the rightful owner of this video.

Next look for "Upload Defaults" and click on it to upload your video you've created.

When a box appears, the descriptions of your video will be displayed inside.

You can add more paragraphs to describe your creation.

For e.g. let people know the location of your Travel Destination, the distinct places of interests and maybe their cultures.

Join Our "Without You Youtube Profits" **Support Group**

Besides this, you need to add interesting text in the text box like the special cuisine in that place, their religions or maybe the myths about what they believe.

Remember to allow people to comment, likes & see your video ratings because its will boosts the popularity of your creation.

The more popular and more likes you have, YouTube will show more ads on your Channel which in turn increases your revenues.

You need to select "Standard YouTube License", and then choose a category which closely matches your video.

In this way your creation will be shown to more people when their searches match your category.

In conclusion, if your Travel video's creations are entertaining, interesting and come with a lot of fun facts on the places of interests you are recommending, the more revenues you'll make consistently every single month.

Likewise the more videos you create and add to your Channel, the more money will be added to your revenue.

P.S.:- Stay tune to Chapter 3 on How to find Viral Video You can use now

Chapter 3 :- Strategies To Find Viral Videos You Can Use Now

This chapter will teach you how to find viral videos.

In order to monetize your video's creation, you need a strategy to find viral videos.

You need to search for videos with a lot of views and followers.

It's important because that kind of video already has a huge audience and when you copy and tweak it to make it your own, you can be sure your video will also get a lot of views.

You can also copy their SEO & Title so that you'll also get recommended on their channel.

To get some ideas of viral videos, I recommend you to search YouTube.

Here's an example of a video that when viral without the creator showing their face.

Amazing Fattest Skill Cutting Big Tree Chainsaw's Machine.

Within a short period of 4 months, it's already got 28M views.

On top of that, it has a good thumbnail to let viewers see a quick snapshot of your video.

Thumbnails are important because it's the first snapshot of your video viewers will see.

You can get interesting thumbnails from Animaker where you can find tons of thumbnails.

Choose one you like and make some changes or add music in the thumbnail background.

After you have uploaded your video, you'll be recommended videos of the same niches by YouTube when you browse for more videos again.

I suggest you subscribe to at least 5 compilation's channels and choose & copy niches or random videos you like to create more of it as your own.

You can find viral videos by looking at its thumbnails, those with a lot of views will definitely worth your efforts to copy and create it as your own.

Do research on Google to get the original clips of the thumbnails and make it a 10 -15 minutes clip but I recommend it to be at least 13 minutes long.

It's because people will think it's common as most YouTube videos are around 10 minutes or longer.

You can add more interesting clips or move boring parts of the video to the rear of the video, and you may add music in the background.

At the end of it, you'll find it very easy to find viral videos, copy and recreate it's to become your own.

Remember to upload all your videos to your own YouTube Channel so that you can leverage on it to make more money for yourself.

Join Our <u>"Without You Youtube Profits"</u> Support Group

There are 2 sites I would like to recommend promoting your video to get viewers:

1 - <u>Sprizzy where it can make your video go viral</u>

2 - <u>Fiverr is worth for you to take a look</u>

P.S.:- Stay tune for Chapter 4:- The Biggest Thumbnails Secrets

Chapter 4:- What are the Biggest Thumbnails Secrets

This chapter will reveal the biggest thumbnail secret nobody ever tells you.

Thumbnails are the first impressions viewers will have when they browse through YouTube.

I'll show you the best thumbnails that nobody ever talks about.

Only 1% of people who are YouTubers will know the importance of thumbnails.

In case some of you might not know what thumbnails, it's basically a snapshot of your video when you post it on YouTube.

These are some good examples of Thumbnails and number of views

When you've a good thumbnail on your video, your CTR (click through rates) will be high.

However, on the first day you posted your video in your Channel, its CTR may not be high, it's alright because not many people have seen it yet.

But you can change your thumbnail after 4 days of your posting and your CTR may be better.

Your video click through rates will correspond to how viral your video will be.

You can check CTR on the analytics of your YouTube Channel.

The higher the CTR the more viewers your video will get, when you have more viewers to your video, definitely you can make more money.

During the first 4 days of your video's posting, most likely your CTR may vary from 10% or lower, it's the average CTR you get on a new video.

However, when you change your thumbnail after 4 days, YouTube may republish your video and it'll likely be going up to a point it can go viral.

It very much depends on the interests your video can generate.

On the other hand I don't want to give you false hope; it may stay around 10% or less.

Never expect your video to go viral overnight, it may happen maybe after a year or more. Or it may not happen at all.

Even your video CTR may not increase, you still have a chance to amend your thumbnail within 28 days.

After that monitor your video because your CTR may get a boost and jump right through to 30% or more which seem to be crazy.

Even a dead video can get blown up and become viral because we'll never know when YouTube algorithms may change and decide to recommend or share your video to more people.

 So sometimes your dead video may have a CTR of less than 3%, do not be disheartened, one fine day, boom it may go viral overnight.

You can always change your thumbnail every 4 days but never change your video title, descriptions and tags.

You have to have all these ready on the day you publish your video.

It's not advisable to change your video title, descriptions and tags because YouTube has already learned your video.

It's known who your viewers are who viewed your video and the CTR.

When you change all these, it'll be confused as to whom they can recommend your video to.

That will be the end of your video's popularity and the downward trend of your CTR.

If you change your thumbnail and expect to get a lot of viewership but it did not happen, it goes to show that it's not good enough or your video concept is not interesting which resulted in not generating a lot of interest around the world.

It can also be that your video's title is not interesting or not catchy enough to catch the eyes of the viewers.

Therefore, it's good to spend time to search for a good thumbnail before you published your video.

After you have changed your thumbnail, you may not get enough CTR but that doesn't matter because you can still change your thumbnail after 28 days.

Even if your video concept is bad but by changing your thumbnail, it may give a boost to your CTR somewhere down the road.

That is how you get to boost your viewership and even get a viral video with high CTR rates after a change of your Thumbnail.

It's just such a simple concept and it really works to help you guys out to get more viewers.

Even if it doesn't work out, just relax and take a look at your thumbnail again, trying to identify what's going wrong.

Remember a good thumbnail is critical for your video to achieve a good CTR rate.

P.S.:- Look out for CTR YouTube Secrets on Chapter 5

Chapter 5:- CTR YouTube Secret

This chapter will let you know what CTR (Click through Rate) is and how important it is.

CTR is when visitors to your YouTube channel click on your video to take a look.

It'll determine how well your video is received & its popularity.

CTR will also determine whether your video is going viral and let you know whether your thumbnail, the topic of your video is bad and maybe your SEO keywords are lacking.

SEO is also dependent on your CTR.

If you have random text or random title which is not related to your video, your video CTR will be a lot lower.

Then YouTube will not recommend it's to people who are constantly browsing for interesting videos.

For example your video title is "Exotic Travel Destination" but the content doesn't describe why the place is so exotic, but instead it just focuses on letting viewers know about the cultures of the people residing in that place.

CTR is the percentage of viewers who were shown the video and clicked on it, one of the good way to get your video noticed is to use Sprizzy

Let's say when you are watching a YouTube video but at the same time you're scrolling through some other videos on the right and do not click on it, it just counts as an impression and not the CTR rates of the video.

CTR happens only when you've clicked on it to watch.

To have a good CTR rate, videos which provide entertainment or give value to people will most likely attract a lot of viewers to click on it.

At the same time, your video thumbnail is equally an important element to have good CTR because there are millions of people browsing through YouTube to look for interesting video contents daily.

If you have a good thumbnail, then most likely more viewers are attracted by your video and the chances of it being viewed is very high which will ultimately increase your video CTR rates.

To find out your video CTR, you need to go to your YouTube Channel's analytics.

Try to monitor your CTR daily in order for you to have some ideas of how your video is performing.

If your CTR is going down daily, you need to take a closer look at the title of your video.

The title of your video may adversely affect the viewership and CTR of your video.

Join Our "Without You Youtube Profits" Support Group

The more eye catching of the video title, it's more likely will correspond to a higher percentage of your CTR.

Secondly, besides the video title, you also need to take care of the retention rate.

If it's constantly going down, you might consider changing your thumbnail.

As mentioned in my previous chapter on thumbnail's secret where I talked about changing your thumbnails after 4 days.

If your CTR or your retention rate is still no good, change your thumbnail again on the 28 days after you have published your video.

One way to make your video CTR blow up is to have a crazy or weird video title.

Likewise you may have trendy topic like this video: -

"Last one to leave the World Hottest Room win $5500").

Join Our "Without You Youtube Profits" Support Group

A very good example of how different video titles, thumbnails and descriptions can make your CTR rate blow up and eventually it went viral.

You can check out vidIQ to get more views and eventually high CTR rates for your video.

To sum up this chapter, remember a viral video has to have good thumbnails, wacky video titles and a good description of your video.

With all these prerequisites it's very hard for your video not to have a very high CTR.

P.S.:- The next chapter 6, I'll talk about Search Engine Optimization (SEO)

Chapter 6 Part I:- Search Engine Optimization (SEO) - Best Tags Tool To Use To Go Viral

Tags is one of the 3 critical components in the **Search Engine Optimization** for your video to go viral.

<u>Rapid Tags</u>

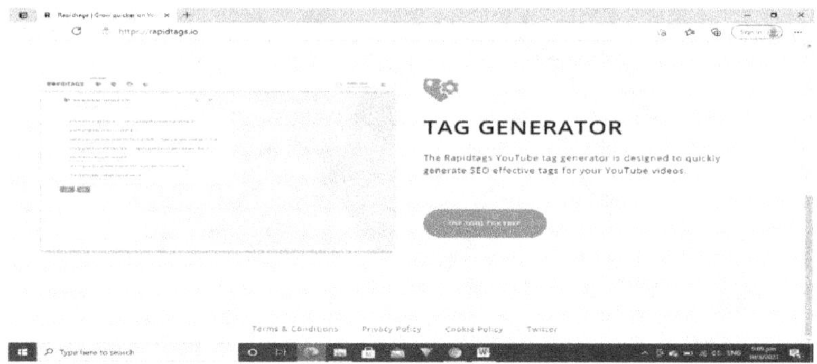

The best tags tool to use is the RapidTags.IO and it's free to use.

Rapid Tags consist of Tags Generator, Tags Analyzer and Tags Ranker.

Tag analyzer will tell you how many views you got on your video, at the same time it will show you estimated views and engagements you got to rank for the challenge.

The minimum views to rank for tags challenge is 63K views. So the more views you have, the higher your ranking on SEO will be.

To use this tool, what you have to do is to copy the title of your video and paste it on the search bar.

Rapid Tags will generate a series of tags related to your video for you to copy and use it on your video.

Tags are important for your video because excellent tags will definitely help your video to be recommended for views and eventually go up the ranking.

All YouTube videos got subscribers count but the total numbers of subscribers are not important anymore.

YouTube will show more of your video if your SEO, watch time rates and CTR are good.

Below is a classics example of a YouTube video using Rapid Tags to generate tags for this video, (Best of NEAR DEATH CAPTURED 2018) which generated more than 9 million views

Join Our _"Without You Youtube Profits"_ Support Group

(Best of NEAR DEATH CAPTURED 2018)

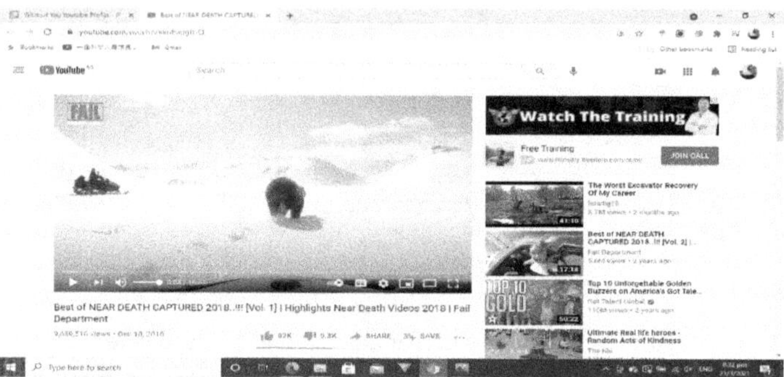

So far Rapid Tags generator is one of the best tag generators around and not many people know about it yet, so I personally recommend all of you to use it.

Chapter 6 Part II:- How To Title Your Video Correctly

The title of your video is the second most important component besides Tags people see on your recommended video or home page of your Channel.

It's important not to use all CAPS titles on your video because it's not authentic and saturated with many YouTube's using all CAPS titles.

People will not see the true title on the video, and they just glance at the title and will not pay attention to the title.

Best of NEAR DEATH CAPTURED 2018

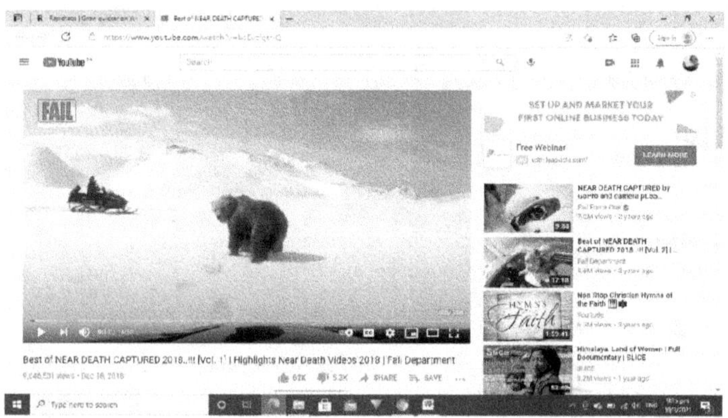

Let me explain why this video (Best of NEAR DEATH CAPTURED 2018) in less than a month got 7 million views.

It's because it didn't use all CAPS in its title but instead it used "Best of" in the beginning of the title followed by all CAPS on the rest.

If the creator uses "BEST OF NEAR DEATH CAPTURED 2018", it'll not seem to be an authentic video and people will not believe it.

However, if you put "Best of" in front of the title, people see that and people know "Near Death" is a compilation of "Near Death Captured" videos.

Obviously they want to see the thumbnails as well.

I think it's not necessary to put the year 2018 there as someone might view this particular video in 2019 which makes the year invalid.

YouTube will only allow 100 characters in a video title, so use your video title wisely.

Letter Count

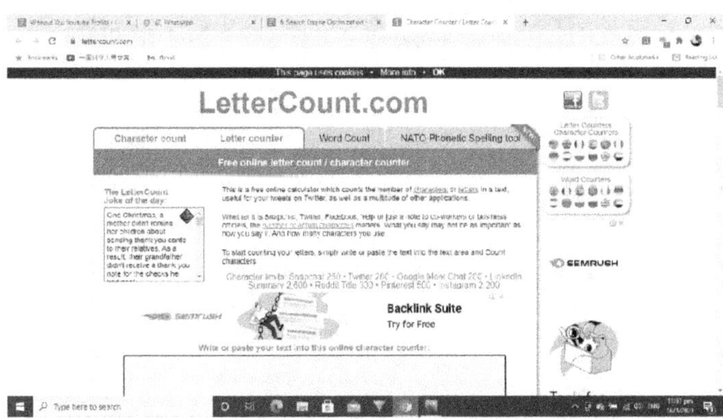

You can checks the number characters of your title using Letter Count

In your video title, you need to emphasize the most important part such as keywords in SEO.

Given the example of the above video, NEAR DEATH is the keywords of the title and it emphasizes the climax of the video which is showing the viewers of a near death situation.

Join Our "Without You Youtube Profits" **Support Group**

Remember not to use all capital letters on the Title.

You can use capital letters for example on "NEAR DEATH" but not on the rest of the title in this video (Best of NEAR DEATH Captured 2018).

Try to use as many keywords or trending keywords as possible like "captured", "near death", "best of and extreme fails".

These are all SEO tags or keywords which are important for your video to have high CTR rates and eventually goes viral.

So it's critical not to use long titles and all capital letters for your video and combining excellence keywords are the keys to make your video go viral.

Chapter 6 Part III:- How to write Descriptions that Boost Views

This chapter will teach you how to use descriptions which will boost your video.

When you will want to describe your video you have just created, try to use tags and keywords with many variations in the title as descriptions.

Most satisfying factory machines and ingenious tools

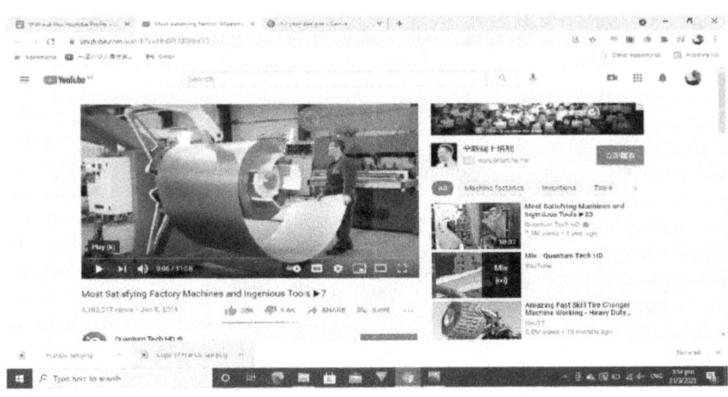

Take a look at this video – Most satisfying factory machines and ingenious tools.

Join Our "Without You Youtube Profits" **Support Group**

The keywords in these video descriptions contain "satisfying", "factory machines" and "ingenious tools" and have many tag variations.

You need to copy it and paste on the Rapid Tags to generate more tags variations and keywords which you can use on your video descriptions.

Tags are single words used in the content of YouTube to describe what the content is.

While keywords are words and phrases are part of the content and are used to identify what the content is all about.

In actual fact, tags and keywords are used in tandem in the descriptions of a video.

You can even add viral video links which garnered millions of views in your descriptions so that when people do a search on it, your video will also get recommended to viewers.

Remember to have all the above 3 components of Tags, Title and Descriptions in your video.

With the combinations of the above 3 components included in your SEO, you can be guaranteed that your video will have a high CTR rate, watch time and attract millions of viewers.

To be rank top in SEO, you may engage the help of Fiverr or TubeBuddy

----

P.S.:- Look out for the next chapter 7 where I'll talk about How to get your video Monetized

Chapter 7:- How to Get Your Video Monetized Quickly

There are many methods for you to get your videos monetized on YouTube.

I'm going to teach you one of the methods to use so that your videos will help you to monetize and make money on YouTube.

First of all, you need to have at least 4000 watch hours or 240K minutes on your video for a period of 1 year in order for you to qualify as a YouTube Partner.

For example most of the videos on YouTube are 3 minutes long, so you will need to have 80K views on your video to monetize.

There is a better strategy to get your video monetized by compilation of videos of an hour.

Compilation Video of an Hour Long

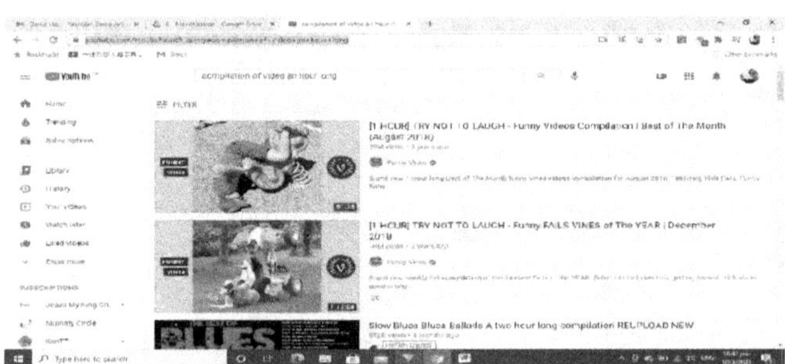

So that after you have edited the video, it may be shortened to around 30 minutes.

With a minimum of 240K minute's views, your video of 30 minutes will only need to get 24K views if each of the viewers stayed for 10 minutes on your video.

In order for you to edit a video of an hour long and not be flagged by YouTube to be duplicating other's videos.

Besides Hit Film Express, I strongly recommend Final Cut Pro X Video Editor to edit your video on Apple iOS.

Just edit and add it your own way and at the same time add your own voice in commentating on the video you are editing.

You don't have to worry about what people think of your comment.

Normally they don't care and will not judge your voice commentating because what they are interested in is the footage of the video.

So when you use your own voice commentating on your compilation video, it's the best way for you not to be flagged as copying other people's video.

Then you can upload it to become your own video.

Normally, you are required to have at least 1000 subscribers for your video in order to qualify for monetization.

You do not have to worry because you can easily attract 1K people to subscribe to your video if it's very interesting or one of a kind video.

But ultimately the numbers of views on your video will determine how much you are paid when ads are shown to viewers.

Buying my little brother every item from A – Z (Expensive)

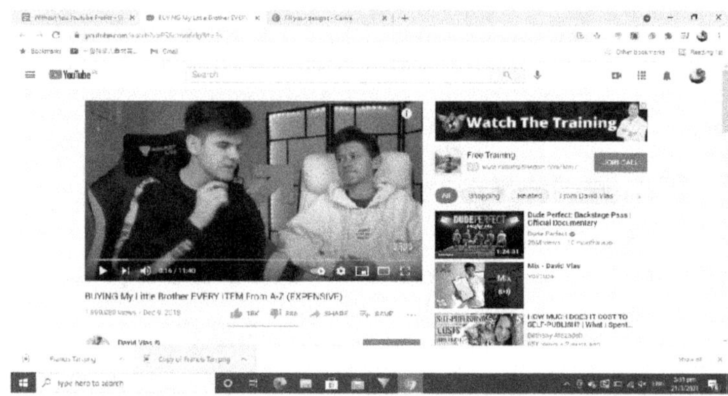

This is also known as the CPM which is cost per 1000 views.

It can range from as little US$0.50 to US$6 based on the location of viewers and the target audience.

Most advertisers pay between US$4 – US$10 per 1000 views but in some cases it may be as low as US$0.10.

It fully depends on the popularity of your videos.

One of the strategies is not to place ads at the beginning but you can place it somewhere between 1.5 minutes to 2.5 minutes of your video.

Join Our "Without You Youtube Profits" Support Group

If your video is about 15 minutes long, I suggest that you can have up to 5 ads for your entire duration of your video.

In this way you will maximize the full potentials of your video and make it a cash cow.

P.S.:- Stay tune to Chapter 8 the final chapter of this eBook is Growing Your YouTube Channel

Chapter 8:- Growing Your YouTube Channel

This chapter will teach you the method on how to gain 1K subscribers in the quickest time.

It doesn't matter whether it's 1K or 10K subscribers in the beginning because after you've published your video; you'll eventually gain more subscribers because of snow ball effects.

It's just a matter of time your subscribers will grow to more than 10K so do not fret over it.

Reddit

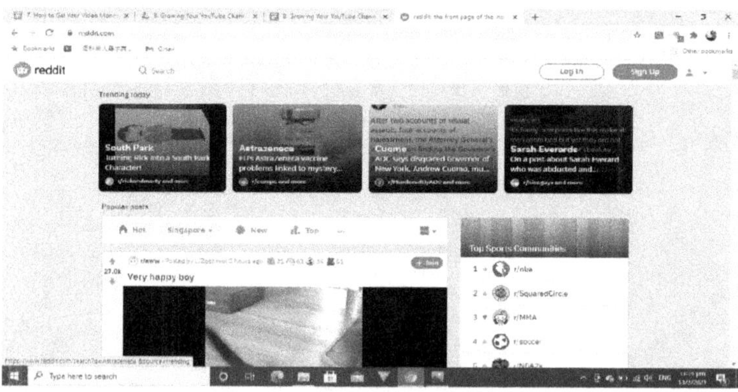

By this time you should have your YouTube Channel ready by now.

Basically, you can go to Reddit/Subreddit to post your video title and its URL.

Reddit is a good place for you to gain a lot of followers to your Channel because they already have more than 200K subscribers.

You need to stand out from the rest of the video creators on Reddit in order for you to gain subscribers easily.

Firstly, you need to create a very unique and eye - catching title for your video.

For e.g. you may want to use   "The most craziest ideas to make money on YouTube"

You do not have to take my ideas but instead use your own creative juices to create one.

Then create a post on the title you have created and add some images which are related to your video's contents.

There are about 19 million users on Reddit so you should be able to gain a lot of followers.

Share Me Now

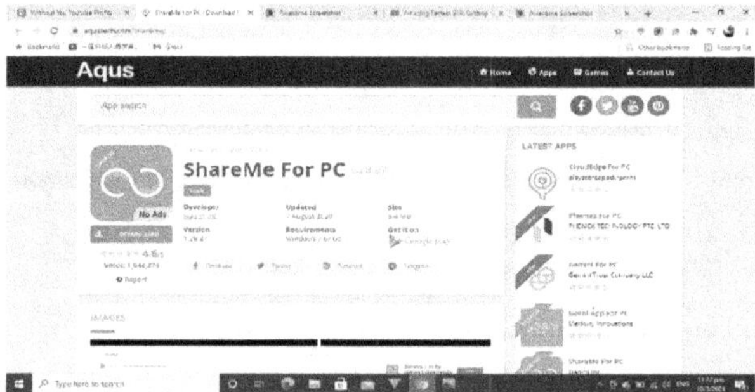

Next you might want to consider using the "Share Me Now" website to promote your videos.

There are already more than 300K users and what you need to do is try to get your video to the top page.

You need to just create an account and then go to the menu to add your account to have your YouTube video ID added.

You can get your YouTube Channel ID when you go to your Channel and copy your URL address to be posted..

You will need to pay a small fee of US$10 for one week, US$14 for 2 weeks or US$95 for a lifetime promoting your Channel on "Share Me Now" to gain more subscribers.

I suggest you pay US$10 for 7 days to try out to get at least 1K subscribers for your video.

Join Our "Without You Youtube Profits" Support Group

It's one of the quickest ways of gaining subscribers if you are new video creators using YouTube compilations.

It's very helpful since you're new to YouTube and your video will be exposed to hundreds of thousand people here.

So that you may monetize your video faster once you can hit 1K subscribers or more easily.

Facebook's YouTube Group

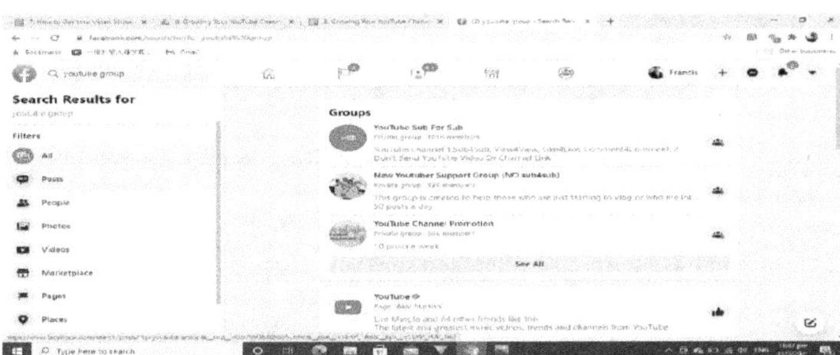

The next best thing to do is going on Facebook and looking for YouTube video's group.

Click on "See All" to get a whole range of YouTube videos listed here.

Just join in as many groups as possible, for example, you can look for the niche videos group or maybe groups with a few hundred thousand members.

It's one of the faster ways to gain followers for your YouTube Channel and it's for free.

Join Our _"Without You Youtube Profits"_ Support Group

Google Ads

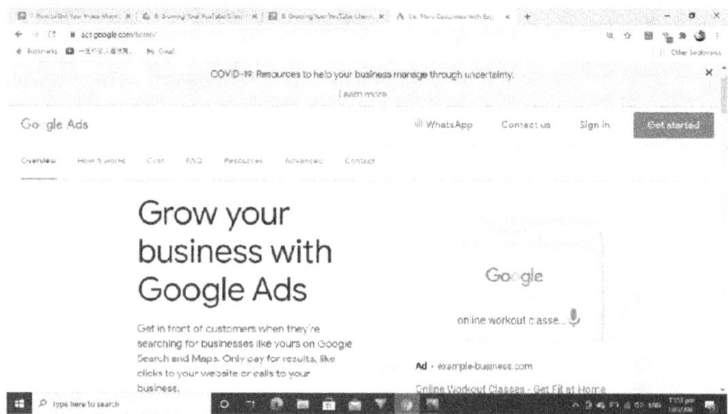

Another way you can grow your YouTube Channel is to promote it on Google using paid Ads.

I think this is the best and fastest way to promote and grow your Channel.

Setup a Google account and select Display ads in order for you to promote your compilation Channel.

Choose Brand Awareness & Reach and add your YouTube Channel URL onto it.

Then click continue to set up to select the country and the language you want to promote your videos.

You need to indicate what you want to focus on, for e.g. high quality traffic.

Look for pay per click and strategy you want to deploy your ads.

Choose maximize conversions so that you can get the highest conversion rates based on your budgets.

Next you need to choose the amount of your budgets for your ads to spend per day.

You can start as little as US$10 per day for your optimizing best performing ads.

Then you need to go on the setting of when you want to commence your ads, whether immediately or you want to schedule a date and time to start.

If you already have a video ready, why you want to delay and wait.

I think you should start immediately so that you can monetize your video straight away.

When you are asked to choose your audiences, you can always set a target audience automatically to make your promotion easier.

As Google will know who are the target audiences for your niche video?

Besides that you need to create a headline for your video.

"Click to watch a funny video" is something like this but eye – catching headlines to generate more interest to your video.

Keep your headline short of up to 30 characters but most important it's an attention grabbing headline.

Lastly add your profile after you have linked your YouTube Channel to your Google account.

Your Channel profile photo will be uploaded to your ads page.

You can also add any image or some image you like to your ads.

Then turns off your ads blocker and boom your video will be automatically uploaded onto your Google ads.

In actual facts, you are targeting 5.1 billion people to reach on Google ads.

However do not forget to prompt viewers to subscribe to your Channel.

Finally you are ready to publish your ads on Google.

The End

P.S.:- I've set up a FaceBook Support Group for you to join so that when you face any difficulties creating your compilation's video, you can get the support you want.

www.ingramcontent.com/pod-product-compliance
Lightning Source LLC
Chambersburg PA
CBHW070531180726
48002CB00022B/2601